TRUST WHAT IS

That which is beyond the senses:

The presence, the stillness, the silence, and
the perceived time and space that allow us to
go beyond. It was never promised to be
easy. Good and bad fortunes are both allies.

Argenis Vegas

I am dedicating this book to you

for making the effort and having the courage and

the willingness to open your heart, even to those

things that you may not understand.

CONTENTS

IN GRATITUDE

I am very grateful to my family; though I did not see it at the time, they were my first teachers. Particularly, thanks to my mother, who always believed in me.

Special thanks to Sensei Koshin Ogui, who opened a window when all the doors were closed. For helping me to find within myself that which I needed, and how to be in chaos and still see its perfection. We both came to the lake and found each other. I am so grateful to have met you.

Thanks to Master Jiru for all he does to make this a better place.

Thanks to Susan Gilkey and Joe Flint for the editing, and Fiona Cook and Ken Burk for believing in this story.

I would like to acknowledge the rich and sustaining network of people and friends who have enhanced and helped me, in one way or another, with the creation and the writing of this book. In no particular order:

Jennifer Bisbing, Mark Contorno, Doug Mitchell,

Imran Omer, Craig Reubelt, Taigen Dan Leighton, Victor Corder, Kathy Kelly, Jill Flanagan, Bill Singerman, Al Haske, Julio Rodriguez, Al Wann, Warren Friesner, Jose De La Cruz, Peter Cherr, Dean Katahira, Gary Weiand, Jim Hampton, Victor Franco, Margaret James, Michelle Rosenaur, Steve Reginald, David Sobeck, Andrea Hazzard and Steve Edfors.

Thanks also to those of you who I am very honored to call my friends.

I DON'T OWN ANYTHING
I don't own anything. I don't own anybody.
I don't even own my body. It's just an instrument
Through which I manifest the expression of my being.
It's impermanent, and I am to treat it well
Be appreciative of it, but not attached to it.
It will one day cease to exist, but what I learn through it shall not.
…If I live in a world of anger, I learn anger
If I live in a world of love, I learn love…
Death, death will come to us no matter what, but life, life is a
miracle.

CHAPTER 1

YOU FIND HELP WHEN IT'S NEEDED

Vancouver, British Columbia, Canada

Present Day

"Where are you going?" his mother asked him.

"I'm going to visit a friend," he responded.

"Don't be late for dinner. Your father will be home around six. We have to talk about your leaving for the university."

"Don't worry, Mom. I'll be back before then," he replied.

When he got to his friend's house, he asked the old man to tell him the story once again before he went away to school. The story had always helped him to open his heart, and to transform his fears into new possibilities.

The young man sat down close to his friend. He was willing to listen even more carefully this time as the old man began.

* * *

Latin America 1950

For the third time, Ana walked into the bedroom to check on her older sister. "Veronica, you've already taken enough time fixing your hair," Ana said hesitantly.

Veronica had been listening to music on the radio and admiring herself in the mirror for forty-five minutes.

Turning off the radio, Veronica told her sarcastically, "Okay, stop rushing me, I'm ready.

You know very well that I don't like to be rushed. Besides, it's always fashionable to be a little late."

"Yes, but Diego told us to be there at eight, and it's already nine thirty," Ana replied.

"Would you please at least put on some lipstick? You look so plain."

"Your lipstick is too red. You know that I don't feel comfortable wearing such a bright color," Ana responded.

As soon as Veronica and Ana arrived at the party, their cousin Diego approached them with his friend Antonio.

"I know you're going to like Veronica," Diego whispered to Antonio, as they got closer to the sisters.

After greeting them with a kiss, Diego introduced them, "Antonio, I'd like you to meet my cousins Veronica and Ana."

It was a warm and beautiful tropical night. The moon was full, illuminating the indoor courtyard of the house where guests were congregated.

Dim lights around the courtyard created a romantic setting that was enhanced by the Carlos Gardel song playing in the background.

The sound of clinking glasses, music playing and people talking gave Ana a great sense of excitement. She had never felt that way before.

Ana thought that Antonio was the most handsome man she had ever met. She felt a little nervous when he leaned over, clasping her shoulders to greet her with a kiss on the cheek. But Antonio's eyes were fixed on Veronica.

Veronica looked very attractive. She was wearing an elegant white dress with red flowers that matched the color of her lipstick. Her long dark wavy hair fell freely down her back.

Ana, on the other hand, was wearing a very simple pink dress with small white dots, and her silky straight black hair was tied back. Her beautiful hazel eyes and lovely face still did not make her look very attractive next to her sister Veronica.

"I like this song; why don't we go inside to dance?" Diego asked them.

Ana immediately grabbed Diego's arm to let him know that she would rather dance with him. Ana was too nervous to even think about dancing with Antonio.

The four of them walked inside the beautiful colonial-style living room. There were already a few other couples on the dance floor. Ana was still holding Diego's arm, so Antonio danced with Veronica.

After a couple of songs, Diego suggested they change partners.

Antonio thought Veronica to be one of the most beautiful girls there that night, but while dancing and talking with her, he found Veronica to be too opinionated and argumentative. Later, after changing partners and having the opportunity to chat with Ana, he found Ana to be more attentive and agreeable than her sister.

Ana's infatuation with Antonio grew with each step. As they danced she felt like her whole body was trembling. She tried to maintain her composure, so he wouldn't notice anything. Her voice cracked a couple of times when she talked to him; she just couldn't help it. In a way, her being so shy made Antonio more at ease.

They all danced, talked, laughed and met other people as the night went on. Later, well past midnight, it got to be too late for the sisters to walk home alone. Antonio had had a little too much to drink, so Diego and his father walked with them to make sure they got home safely.

That night was unforgettable for Ana. Thoughts of Antonio occupied her mind. She couldn't stop thinking about Antonio. She talked about him with her mother constantly.

Her mother finally said, "You hardly know this man, and you go on talking about him, as if you have known him for years. According to your sister, he doesn't have a good reputation. He's known to be a flirt and a drinker, who loves to go from bar to bar. What kind of future could you have with a man like that?"

With a look of sadness in her eyes, Ana replied, "Mom, Veronica doesn't really know him!"

Ana didn't know how well her sister knew Antonio, but she wanted her mother to approve of him.

The next time Ana saw Antonio she was at the
market with Veronica. She saw him walking
towards her, as she was waiting for Veronica to
finish buying a few more items. She frantically
tried to fix her hair and dress while she was still
clutching the grocery bag. Just as Antonio looked
up and saw her, some of the groceries fell, and
Antonio walked over to help her pick them up.

Ana's heart skipped a beat and the blood rushed to
her head. She couldn't hide the emotion that she
was feeling inside.

Though she couldn't look him in the eye, she
managed to say, "Oh, thank you, Antonio."

"Do we know each other?" he asked.

Her heart sunk. "Yes, we met at my cousin
Diego's party three weeks ago." She tried to hide
the fact that she was crestfallen. He had not even
remembered her.

"Oh yes, you're Veronica's younger sister. What
was your name again?"

"Ana, my name is Ana," she replied with a forced

smile.

"Nice to see you again, and please say hello to your sister," he told her, as he continued on his way.

"Who was that?" Veronica asked her when she returned.

"Antonio, the guy we met at Diego's party, remember?"

"Oh, him, the Casanova. The one you cannot stop talking about. Well, if you truly want him to notice, you'll need to spend a little more time on your appearance."

Since Antonio had obviously forgotten her, Ana considered her sister's advice, she thought, 'I could do something prettier with my hair, wear a little makeup, and pay more attention to the way I dress.'

After that meeting at the market, Ana kept running into Antonio and give a polite hello and pass quickly by. She was always careful to look her best, as her sister had suggested. She also walked more frequently around town, hoping to see the man she could not get out of her mind.

One afternoon, as she was returning home from an errand for her mother, she saw Antonio sitting on a bench at the plaza. This time, after greeting him, she found the courage to stop and talk.

Antonio had started to notice Ana. Her beautiful hazel eyes enchanted him as he talked to her. Her eyes were sparkling in the sun, as the light illuminated them. He couldn't resist and told her, "You really have some beautiful eyes."

She blushed, but managed to say, "Thank you! I'm glad you like them."

She spent most of that afternoon talking to him. He spoke of all his dreams and goals. Antonio enjoyed her attention. It occurred to him that she would make a "perfect wife". When he watched other women walking by, Ana didn't seem to mind. This had never happened to him with other girls—they always shot him a nasty look. It appeared that she was not very demanding which would allow him his freedom.

As they were talking, she suddenly realized that her mother was waiting for her.

"I'm so sorry, but I must go now. My mother is waiting for me to get home. Thank you! I've really enjoyed talking to you," she told him, as she got up.

Antonio offered to walk her home, so they could continue talking. Ana found it easy to talk to him, despite her shyness. As they approached Ana's house, Antonio gave her a kiss on the cheek and asked to see her again at the plaza the following Sunday afternoon. She agreed, and then stood watching Antonio until he turned the corner.

As she entered the house, her mother reprimanded, "Why are you so late? And who was that man you were talking to outside?"

Ana apologized for being so late, and told her that the guy was Antonio, Diego's friend.

Ana was thrilled with her plans for the following Sunday. She asked her mother to help her with a dress she was sewing, not noticing that her mother was very upset.

"Ana, you're not even listening to me, but just thinking about that boy. Your father will be here in a few minutes and I haven't been able to get things ready for dinner waiting for you."

"I apologize, Mom. I'm very sorry that I took so long," she said, and started to set the table.

The next day, she and her mother finished the dress. It fit perfectly. "You look beautiful!" exclaimed her mother.

"Thanks, Mom," Ana responded, and gave her mother a kiss, as she was trying on her new dress.

"Mom, I think I need to do something different with my hair, so he'll notice something different, don't you think?" Ana asked her mother while looking at herself in the mirror.

Veronica, overhearing the conversation, said, "Why don't you cut off your nose? For sure he'll notice that."

Ana was used to her sister's sarcasm, so she completely ignored the comment, and asked Veronica to please let her use some of her makeup.

Veronica replied, "No, because you don't even know how to put it on! You will end up looking like a clown. Besides, I don't want you using my stuff."

"Please Veronica, I won't be using very much, and you can help me put it on, please, please," Ana begged her.

"Okay, I'll help you, but stop begging. I can't stand people begging," Veronica said, as she got up and went into the kitchen.

That Sunday afternoon when Ana got to the plaza Antonio was already there waiting for her. He did notice her flattering hairstyle, makeup and her new dress.

"You look very pretty," he told her, as he got up and gave her a kiss on her cheek.

"Thank you," she responded, as she also gave him a greeting kiss.

He invited her to a nearby coffee shop. They sat on the patio of the cafe. They talked and laughed and spent all that afternoon together. Now Antonio, without realizing it, was falling for Ana.

From then on, he and Ana were together every Sunday afternoon.

One of those afternoons, Antonio told her that he had a surprise for her. He took her over to the house where he was renting a room. He opened the door of the room, and there was a single bed and a sink with a small mirror above it. In one corner there was a metal rack bolted from wall to wall with a couple of shirts and some pants hanging on it.

Ana noticed something in the other corner covered with a white sheet, and asked him what that was. He told her that it was her surprise, and that she should uncover it. Ana did as Antonio suggested, and underneath the sheet were a table and four chairs.

"This is my first wedding present to you," Antonio said smiling.

Ana could not wait to get home to tell her mother what Antonio had already bought her for when they got married.

When Ana got home, she was so excited that she mistakenly told her mother, "Antonio bought me four tables and a chair."

Her mother asked, "Don't you think that things

are moving a little too fast? And why would he buy four tables and only one chair?"

Veronica, who was nearby painting her fingernails, said to their mother, "It's very clear to me, Mom. I'm sure he's planning to open up a restaurant with her, don't you think?"

Ana calmly turned to Veronica with a sense of curiosity and seriousness at the same time, and asked her, "Veronica, why do you always like to put me down? Does it give you some sense of satisfaction?"

Their mother laughed, when she heard what Ana had asked her sister. She had never heard Ana challenge Veronica in that way before.

"Ana, where did that come from?" her mother asked her, as she continued to laugh.

"Oh, please," Veronica said.

Ana turned around and looked at her mother and they both broke down laughing. They all knew that there was a core of truth in what Ana had said. Feeling somewhat upset and embarrassed by the situation, Veronica got up and left the room, while Ana and their mother kept laughing.

The next time Ana and Antonio met, they went on a picnic. Ana prepared a basket with two sandwiches and a couple of apples. Antonio brought a bottle of wine, two glasses and a blanket.

They walked a long way up the mountain, until they found a shady spot with a spectacular view. They were already feeling hungry after the long walk, but Ana wanted to look over the cliff to see the town. As she stood there, she felt the wind blowing through her hair. She took a deep breath, filling her lungs with the fresh air and the energy of the mountain.

Antonio came up behind her, put his arms around her and gave her a soft kiss on the cheek. Ana turned around and met his embrace. For the first time their lips met. At that moment, they felt like the whole world belonged to them.

There was not another soul around the place, only the wind blowing and birds singing could be heard.

Later, they ate, drank, talked, kissed and fell

asleep in each other's arms.

When Ana awoke, it was late and getting dark. She quickly woke Antonio and started packing. She was worried that if they didn't leave soon, they wouldn't find their way back in the dark.

They headed down the path, but quickly realized they weren't sure it was the same way they had come up. They kept walking, hoping that they were going in the right direction. It was already too dark to see their way clearly. Ana was afraid, and the eerie sounds of the creatures of the night in the brush heightened her fear. They both felt very cold.

Ana asked Antonio to please stop for one second. They put everything down and she grabbed both of his hands and looked up and prayed, "Lord, please help us find our way." Then, they picked everything back up and continued walking.

Not very long after Ana's prayer, they noticed a dim light in the distance. They walked towards it and saw a little house. Then they knew for sure that they were lost, because they had not seen that little house on their way up.

"How surprising someone living here, in the middle of nowhere," Antonio said.

They could see the light of a lantern shining through a window of the small house.

Antonio knocked on the wooden door, and a few seconds later they heard footsteps.

An old man opened the door with a lantern in his hand. He seemed like a character from a movie. He was dressed in old clothing, but looked very clean. He had deep brown eyes, almost black. The lamp's light reflection in his eyes made them feel like he could almost see through them.

"Sir, we're lost and we need some help to find our way back to town," Antonio said.

Without saying a word, the old man set off walking through the woods down the mountain, and Ana and Antonio followed him. Though the man seemed a little strange and out of place, they felt that they could trust him.

He led them until they were at the outskirts of town and able to continue on their own. Then, before they could even thank him, he disappeared into the darkness.

The whole experience with the old man seemed like a foggy dream. He was there to guide and help them, without even expecting a thank you in return.

Ana returned several times to look for the old man to thank him, but was never able to find him. The last time she went was shortly after she and Antonio were married. Again, she was not able to find him or the little house.

"I guess you find help when it's needed, that's all," Ana told her new husband.

THE WHOLE AND THE ONE
I am the whole that has been divided,
And the one that belongs to all things.

CHAPTER 2

WORRYING IS NEVER FRUITFUL

Fifteen years later —1965

Time went by swiftly and the kids grew older. Antonio worked hard to make ends meet as a factory worker. He dreamed of becoming a lawyer, but never had a formal education.

He was becoming more frustrated with his life, his job and resented his marriage and children. Ana, on the other hand, was a very loving, caring and attentive mother and wife.

Every Friday after work, Antonio and his friends went out drinking at a local bar. He often came home drunk. This usually led to arguments with Ana about the kids or anything else Antonio found to complain about to Ana.

On one such Friday night, Antonio came home especially drunk. He stumbled and fell towards his son Alejandro, who was doing his homework at the dining room table. He caught his balance and screamed, "Get out of here, before I hit you and send you flying across the room!"

Ana stopped ironing and immediately got between them to protect Alejandro.

"You would have to go over my dead body before touching him or any of them in that condition," Ana said calmly, but with a fierce look that let him know she was serious.

Alejandro quickly ran into the bedroom. At the entrance, he found his brother Pedro crying. "Quit your blubbering, and go to bed," Alejandro scolded him, as he fought back his own tears.

The other boys were already in bed, scared and listening to their parents arguing.

"Yes, protect them, that's why they're useless and good for nothing. Do you think you're going to be able to protect them all their lives? In this world, they're going to have to work hard and learn to defend themselves to survive, like I do. You're just raising a bunch of fools. You think that they're going to go to school to become doctors and lawyers. How do you think we are going to pay for it? And they are dumb anyway.

"My father died when I was two years old, and I've been working as long as I can remember. Now I have to support all of you. They all should go out and get a job and earn a living," Antonio yelled to Ana, as he went into the bedroom.

At the moment that Ana entered their bedroom, Antonio angrily punched and cracked the mirror of a small medicine cabinet hanging on the wall. Seconds later, he noticed that he had cut his hand. Then, he furiously pulled the cabinet off the wall and threw it down. It shattered all over the floor.

Hearing the commotion and breaking glass, Alejandro and Pedro jumped out of bed, terrified that something might have happened to their mother. They crawled to the other room and carefully peeked underneath the curtain, hanging at the entrance of their parents' bedroom. When they saw the broken glass, the medicine cabinet on the floor and their mother's feet walking towards the dresser, they quickly got up and ran back to bed.

The other kids asked what had happened. Alejandro quietly said, "Nothing. Go back to bed."

"You can break everything in this house, but you cannot touch any of us. You better have that very clear in your head," Ana said firmly, as she took a piece of cloth from a drawer to bandage his hand.

As Ana reached for his hand, Antonio screamed, "Leave me alone and go away; I don't need you or anybody to help me."

"Do you want the whole neighborhood to hear you? What are they going to think?" she cried.

Antonio yelled even louder, "I don't care what they think. They don't pay my damn bills."

Ana, concerned that the neighbors would hear, asked him to please lower his voice.

Antonio sat at the edge of the bed, his hand still bleeding. The earlier drinking, emotions from the argument, and pain from his hand came over him all at once. He was now exhausted, drifting off to sleep while still sitting, mumbling to himself.

Ana gently pushed him down onto the pillow. She cleaned and bandaged his hand, straightened him out, took off his shoes and kissed him on the forehead.

The next day, their son Pedro went out for a walk up the mountain.

Once alone in the forest, the fear, insecurity and anxiety that he felt the night before were completely disappearing. Being surrounded by nature allowed him to connect with a completely different world from the one he knew with his family.

He kept walking, enjoying everything that was happening around him—butterflies flying from flower to flower, wind blowing, birds singing, water flowing down the creek, and ants marching in harmony in a single line carrying leaves to their nest.

Pedro knelt to observe the ants, then he thought, how wonderful it would be if his family could be just like the ants. They helped each other, rather than fighting, yelling and hurting one another. They worked together to make the best nest, where they all could be protected and nurtured.

To Pedro, the ants seemed to clearly understand what a family was all about.

'What a wonderful world,' he thought. He wished his father could see and understand that. "Why can't we be like the ants?" he said to himself quietly.

He continued walking and enjoying the feeling of being alone in the woods, everything around him seemed to be so alive. The branches of the trees were swaying in the wind, as though dancing to the singing of the birds.

As he was walking, he saw a small wooden house. He didn't remember seeing a house before on that part of the mountain.

The little house had a small corral with a few chickens, a goat and some pigeons flying around. There were also a few cages with birds. The cages were hanging on the fence of the corral.

As he approached, he saw a parrot on top one of the cages.

The parrot was saying, "Lorenzo, Lorenzo!"

Pedro got closer to the bird and said, "Oh, your name is Lorenzo. Mine is Pedro."

As he was talking to the bird, Pedro heard someone approaching. He turned around and saw an old man.

"I didn't know anybody lived here," Pedro called.

The old man walked past Pedro, as if he wasn't even there, went into the little hut and let the door shut behind him.

He was carrying a fishing cane and a few fish in an old beat up metal bucket. The sea was about a two hours' walk on the other side of the mountain.

Pedro crossed and rested his arms on the fence of the corral, and raising his voice to make sure that the old man would hear him, said, "Mister, do you like to fish?"

Since he didn't get a response from the old man, he said, "I like it here. My name is Pedro. What's your name, sir?"

He got no response. After a moment, Pedro told him, "Since I don't know your name, I'll call you Don Gregorio. It's the middle name of one of my mother's favorite saints. Every time one of us gets sick, she always talks to him. She says, "Please, Jose Gregorio Hernandez help my son to get well soon." After that, we always do get well. It's like he comes to help us, so she won't worry.

"My mother also loves Mother Mary, and of course Jesus. We always go to church during the Holy Week. One time, during the procession while holding a candle, I burned myself. The wax dripped all over my arm. It really hurt!

Pedro waited for a while to see if the old man would say something.

"Well, I guess you don't feel like talking. I'm going to leave now, but will come back tomorrow to visit you again," he promised the old man and left.

When Pedro returned the following day, he didn't see the old man anywhere and he noticed that the goat was out of the corral.

Pedro patted the goat and gave it a kiss on the head, as he went by it walking towards the house. He cautiously pulled the door open to look inside the house. When he turned his head to the left side corner not far from the door, he saw the old man lying on a small wooden bed. He appeared ill, so Pedro walked in to make sure he was alright.

Don Gregorio opened his eyes, as Pedro neared. "Oh, it's you again," he said, in a deep, scratchy and weak voice. "Do me a favor and get that brown bottle up on the shelf next to the stove."

Pedro turned nervously and saw the bottle on a high shelf.

Pedro grabbed a wooden stool next to an old table, both of which were probably made by the old man, to reach for the bottle.

"What is it?" Pedro asked, as he walked back with the bottle in his hand.

"Never mind, just open it, pour half a cup and give it to me," Don Gregorio said, hardly having the energy to finish speaking.

"This smells really bad, are you sure you want to drink this?" Pedro asked him, after opening the bottle.

"Just do as I say," Don Gregorio told him in a weak voice.

"Maybe I should bring my mother to come to help you. She knows a lot about these things," Pedro said with a concerned look in his eyes.

The old man almost sat up and then immediately fell back on the bed. He was just able to whisper, "You will do no such a thing."

Pedro, scared that Don Gregorio would hurt himself, did as he asked him. He poured half a cup of the nasty-smelling liquid into a metal cup he found on a crate next to Don Gregorio's bed.

Don Gregorio drank it all, and then told Pedro to go home and let him sleep.

Pedro walked back and sat on the stool. He waited for a little while, until Don Gregorio was completely asleep, then quietly approached him and whispered to him, "I'll be back tomorrow."

The old man mumbled something in his sleep, turning to one side.

Pedro went outside and opened the corral gate. He guided the goat into the corral and then closed and latched the gate.

That evening Pedro had a hard time falling asleep

thinking about the old man, sick and all alone in the woods. The next day, he couldn't wait for school to be over, so he could go to see his friend.

Pedro was out of breath from his hurried climb when he got to Don Gregorio's house that afternoon. Slowly he pulled open the rough, hand-made door in order not to disturb Don Gregorio, in case he should be asleep.

He took a look inside and noticed that the old man was no longer in bed, and that there were some dirty dishes on the table. He then heard some noise outside and stepped out and saw him. The old man was repairing a hole in the fence at the back of the corral.

'That must have been how the goat got out yesterday,' Pedro thought.

"I was worried about you, and wanted to see how you were," he said to Don Gregorio.

"Worrying is never fruitful," Don Gregorio told him.

"Please tell that to my mother. She worries about everything and everyone. If something happens to someone, it is like it happened to her.

"Well, I see you are doing much better. That nasty-smelling liquid must be a powerful thing," Pedro said, grinning, happy to see the old man doing well.

"I need to go home now because I stayed out too late yesterday, and I don't want my mother to worry. I'll come back after school tomorrow," Pedro promised him, as he headed out.

Pedro continued visiting Don Gregorio every afternoon after he had finished his homework. It felt like a reward. To Pedro, just sitting and watching the animals gave him a great sense of peace and joy. He would sit on an old ladder resting against the mango tree and watch them for long periods of time.

His favorites were the pigeons. He became familiar with every one of them and their nesting sites. He gave each one a saint's name. The couple occupying the nest closest to the door of the corral was Mary and Joseph.

There were always a couple of babies in each nest. Their nests were built on the sidewall of the house, covered by a roof, inside the corral. He would use the ladder to look in and check on the babies. He loved to watch the parents feeding them and the courting dance of the males.

His mother once asked him, "Do you know what the male pigeon says to the female?"

"No," he responded.

"Juan Felipe loves you, Juan Felipe loves you." That was his mother's interpretation of what the male pigeon said to the female, as it danced around her.

Pedro laughed every time he heard his mother imitating the male pigeon.

'Who needs Disneyland when I have my mother, Don Gregorio, and all the animals that make me so happy?' Pedro thought one afternoon as he was coming back home from visiting Don Gregorio.

THE SOURCE
I am the source
I am the source of my own feelings
I am the source of my own experiences
I am the source of my own misery
I am the source of my own joy
I am the source of my own creation
I am the source
I am the source.

CHAPTER 3

ANYTHING IS POSSIBLE

"Don Gregorio, Don Gregorio," Pedro called excitedly, as he saw the old man returning from his fishing trip.

Don Gregorio had been gone for at least two hours. He left in a small, old boat that he must have motorized himself.

Pedro had walked with Don Gregorio to the seaside very early that morning.

This was Pedro's first time seeing the ocean, even though it was just on the other side of the mountain. His family never went, for fear of getting lost and because it seemed too far away.

Pedro ran along the beach with his arms open, as if he were flying. The birds scattered in the sky like they were flying along with him. As he continued to run, he saw them getting further and further away from him, until they were lost in the distance.

Pedro didn't want to go too deep into the water because his mother had once told him about almost drowning when she was a little girl.

As he was walking back, he started picking up seashells and putting them into his pocket. When he got closer to the entrance of the path, marked by some big rocks, he got down on the ground. Playing in the sand, he dug an elaborate tunnel. It had three different exits with two strong pillars on each side of the main entrance.

Later, he climbed on the rocks. Trying to walk on top of the rocks, he almost lost his balance, but quickly recovered. He continued to walk very carefully until he reached the edge of the biggest rock. He sat where he could see the ground below him and watched the waves, as he waited for his friend to return.

The waves changed as they washed ashore. *Comings and goings....* There was a constant movement, nothing ever stayed the same. The waves varied according to the weather conditions and seabed. Some waves seemed so much bigger than others, but regardless of how big or small, they all ended up at shore, retreating back into the great mass of water.

Pedro looked down and gazed at the ground below him. He remained silent and still for a while. Suddenly, he had a brief flash. He had a profound sense of being everything. It felt as if he had merged into all things and disappeared. But, at the same time, he felt intensely alive and vibrant.

He had a feeling of vastness and freedom. He didn't know or understand what had happened. But, whatever it was, it gave him the realization that he could be and do anything. Nothing was impossible.

He felt shaken, and a little bit afraid.

Pedro ran out into the water to reach the boat,

once he saw Don Gregorio closer to shore. He was relieved to see someone familiar after that strange feeling.

The old man gave him the fishing pole and the bucket containing the fish, then pulled the boat out of the water.

They dragged the boat into a ditch in the woods and covered it with a dark green tarp and some branches that helped camouflage it.

Soon after that, they were on their way back to the house.

As they walked, Pedro thought and asked Don Gregorio, "What do you think of a boy liking another boy, is there anything wrong with that?"

Pedro was nine years old, and he was already aware of his attraction to other boys. He knew he was a little different from his brothers and friends.

"Pedro, just because people don't understand something doesn't mean that it's wrong. And it doesn't mean that people are wrong for not understanding. They just simply don't understand it."

"I know, I just wish it wasn't like that," Pedro replied.

"Is there a boy that you like?"

"Yes," he responded.

"Have you told him that you like him?"

Pedro, with a panicked look on his face said, "No! He's older than I am and he would hit me! One time after school I was looking at him, and he asked me why I was staring. I told him that I was not staring, and ran home.

"I think he already knows that I like him. I'm afraid he will tell his friends and they'll make fun of me and beat me up.

"Already at school some kids call me a sissy because I don't like to fight. I don't understand why they always want to fight and why they want to hurt and make fun of me."

After that, Pedro remained silent for the rest of the way.

When they got to Don Gregorio's house, Pedro said good-bye and ran.

It was past seven o'clock when he got home.

"Where were you, Pedro? I was dead worried about you. You have been gone all day!"

"Do you know what time it is?" his mother asked him.

"I'm so sorry, Mom. I went to the seaside and it was so beautiful! I really didn't know it was going to take that long, honestly," he told his mother apologetically.

"For goodness' sake Pedro, all by yourself?" she asked with a concerned look on her face.

"Sort of," he replied.

Pedro knew how to compromise not to lie to his mother, but something told him not to mention Don Gregorio.

"How could you do that Pedro? You could have gotten lost."

"Mom, sometimes we know things that we really don't."

"Pedro, please stop talking like that, and don't you ever do that again," she told him firmly.

"I'm sorry to have worried you, Mom," he apologized again.

But, Pedro did not tell his mother that he would not do it again. He believed that all his family's fears and insecurities were only limiting and not real.

'There was no danger in going to the other side,' he thought. But at the same time, he wanted to be understanding and respectful of his mother.

That night, as his mother was getting all the clothes together to be washed, she found the seashells in Pedro's pocket. The next morning, Pedro found them cleaned and neatly placed together on the nightstand next to his bed. He smiled as he saw them.

A few days later, while visiting Don Gregorio, Pedro looked away from watching the birds. He saw the old man repairing storm damage done to the roof of the house by a fallen tree branch.

Don Gregorio worked as if Pedro were not even there. He was completely focused on his task. It was as if the outside world didn't even exist. It was delightful to watch the old man working.

Pedro sat and observed him. He saw how mindfully Don Gregorio performed every action.

Everything seemed to flow as the old man worked. Pedro guessed that there must be something important about the way one moves to do a good job. But, he didn't know what.

When he saw an opportunity, Pedro asked, "Have you ever thought that anything is possible?"

After a period of silence, Don Gregorio finally answered by asking him, "What do you mean?"

Pedro took a moment to think, and responded, "I think that anything you can think of or dream about, you can actually do."

"Then, that is true for you," Don Gregorio said.

"But not many people think that way," Pedro said, anxiously hoping that Don Gregorio would say something more.

"Whatever can be conceived in the mind can be manifested in life, if the conditions are right for that to be manifested," Pedro heard the old man say, as he watched him put away the working tools.

"But my Dad says that if you are poor, you will always be poor, and you'll never be able to go to the University. He says the University is only for rich folks, and the only way to get ahead in life is to take advantage of other people."

"Then, that is true for him," Don Gregorio responded.

Pedro paused and later said, "I guess you do have to have money to go to the University and do things like that. But I would really like to graduate from the University one day," he said to Don Gregorio.

"Your willingness can get you there," Don Gregorio replied.

"Willingness, what do you mean by that?" Pedro asked.

"A pianist cannot be a great pianist just by having the greatest teachers, the most beautiful piano and the most wonderful music to play. Her willingness alone could make her a great pianist. Use your willingness to undo or go beyond your own personal will. Always do your best and let it go, without being attached to any particular outcome or result. Then the rest will just appear."

"What if it's something that I really want?" Pedro asked.

"Sometimes what you want is not what is best for you, but 'what is' always is.... Your source knows more than your thinking mind. That source is essentially you, but yet bigger than you. It's like the wave dissolving into the ocean and becoming the ocean itself. The wave is never separate from the ocean. The wave named Pedro is just an expression of that ocean. You're too little to see this yet, but you will someday," Don Gregorio told him.

It was kind of funny to Pedro that the old man used a comparison to the ocean. After all, it was at the seaside he had that strange experience and realization, as he watched the waves and later sat still and remained silent looking at the ground.

It was getting late, and Pedro knew his mother would worry. He felt reassurance and comfort after hearing what Don Gregorio had to say. Then, it occurred to him that nobody in town believed that he even existed.

"Is Don Gregorio even for real? Or is he just my imagination?" Pedro questioned himself.

Pedro didn't even know Don Gregorio's real name.

Pedro had overheard a neighbor saying, "Pedro is such a nice kid, but he goes alone up the hill and sits there to watch the birds. He also talks about this Don Gregorio, who is supposed to live up there.

"I hope there is nothing wrong with him. Sometimes he doesn't behave like the rest of the children. He likes to hang around older people rather than kids of his own age."

After hearing that conversation, Pedro was careful not to let people see him when he went to visit Don Gregorio. He kept Don Gregorio a secret after that.

Pedro was always the first of the kids to get up after his father had gone to work. That was his private time with his mother. He loved spending that morning time with her. It was the only time he had her all to himself.

They always had something to talk about, and most times his mother would make him laugh.

Early one morning, while he was helping her prepare breakfast, she told him, "You'd better be careful not to spend so much time alone in the woods. What about if something happens to you? That mountain can be a dangerous place. Your father and I got lost there once, when we were younger. Only with the help of an old man, were we able to find our way back."

"What did the old man look like?" Pedro asked.

"He was like a mystery man. There was something special about him," she said as she thought.

"He had piercing black eyes and very dark complexion. His curly white hair looked like snowfall at the top of a mountain. I believe he was an angel," his mother said with a dreamy look on her face.

Pedro now had no doubt that the old man, who had helped his parents long ago, was Don Gregorio. But, he did not say anything to his mother.

"I'm not doing anything wrong, Mom. I just like going out for a walk," he replied.

"I know, my son. I just worry about you spending so much time alone, and talking about this Don Gregorio, who nobody knows," she said concerned.

Pedro was happy that he did not mention Don Gregorio's name, after his mother said that.

"I promise I won't talk about him anymore," he told her with a smile.

"It's time for your brothers to get ready to go to school," she said.

Pedro dreaded the task of waking them up. It was never easy.

Pedro was so tired of fighting to get them up. On sudden impulse, he grabbed a glass of water and sprinkled it on their faces and ran, and it worked!

"They are up, Mom," he said, as he grabbed his books, and left as fast as he could before they were able to reach him.

"Those boys are truly afraid of water," he said to

himself and laughed on his way to school that day.

After that, it became easier to get them up by threatening them with water. They would get furious and get up to go after him.

'I wish I had thought of this sooner,' Pedro thought with a smile on his face.

With a glass in his hand, even if it were empty, Pedro would tell them with a grin on his face, "Here I come boys! It's time to wake up. It's get up or water, so you choose.

"I think, I would pick to get up," he would say and ran every time they would try to go after him.

"Thank God for water," he said to himself and laughed.

THE PAIN OF LIFE
The pain of life is going to carry me
Where simplicity is the essence of all existence.

CHAPTER 4

YOU ARE THE ONLY ONE YOU WILL EVER BE ABLE TO CHANGE

Pedro left home at fifteen.

He stayed with different relatives who lived near the high school he wanted to attend.

Leaving all the family problems and arguments behind was a very important step.

After he graduated, he worked as a government clerk during the day, and attended the university at night.

His Aunt Veronica, with whom he was staying at the time, waited up for him to come home from class. She always had something warm for him to eat. Pedro and his aunt talked and laughed together. They shared a special closeness.

One Saturday morning, as Pedro was leaving for his regular weekend visit to his family, he heard his cousin Patricia talking to her mother.

Patricia, who was pregnant, said to her mother, "I don't know where Pedro will go now Mom, but I'll need that room once the baby is born."

After hearing that, Pedro realized he would have to move again, but he didn't know where this time.

That Saturday evening, while Pedro was studying at his parents' home, he heard his brother Roberto arguing with their mother in the kitchen.

"I told you I needed that shirt clean to go out tonight," Roberto shouted.

"I forgot it, my son, I'm sorry. I'll have it ready for you," Ana apologized.

"Yes, you're going to do a magic act, right? I need it right now. Just forget it," Roberto said, storming out of the kitchen.

"If you knew you needed that shirt clean, why didn't you wash it yourself?" Pedro called to him.

Roberto rushed over to where Pedro was sitting, and pointing his finger at Pedro's face said, "Just you mind your own business."

Pedro stood up. "And if I don't, what are you going to do about it?"

Roberto pushed Pedro hard on the shoulders, nearly making him fall. Pedro recovered and was about to push back, when Ana came and softly slapped him. "Pedro, stop that!" she said.

Pedro quietly went into the bedroom, and sat at the edge of the bed.

"Every time he comes here it's nothing but trouble. Why does he have to come here and tell everybody what to do? Doesn't he have anything better to do?" Roberto yelled out loud deliberately so Pedro could hear.

"This isn't his house anymore anyway," Roberto said, as he threw the door open knocking it against the wall and walked out.

Ana came into the bedroom and sat next to Pedro. They remained silent for a while.

"I'm so sorry my son, but I had to do something

to prevent you from getting into a fight with your brother," Ana finally said to Pedro, in a soft and loving voice.

Pedro looked down at his hands, and said to her, "They all treat you like a slave, and expect you to do everything for them. They don't want to work or go to school. They just want to have fun.

"Dad comes home drunk every Friday night. He yells and screams, so the whole world can hear him, and breaks anything that gets in his way.

"Alejandro keeps you up late at night on the weekends, worrying about him, while he parties all night long and gets drunk.

"What kind of life is this, Mom? Thank God, at least Maria Elena and Marcos don't live here," his voice was cracking and tears had started running down his face, as he kept looking down.

Maria Elena was the first and only daughter. Ana was very ill after Maria Elena's birth and was hospitalized for some time. Antonio's sister, Guadalupe, cared for the baby while Ana was recuperating.

The baby was never returned home to her mother. Guadalupe, who had lost her daughter in a car accident and could not have any more children, would get severely sick and depressed every time that Ana tried to get her child back. Maria Elena was kept and raised by Guadalupe, which caused Ana great pain and sorrow.

Marcos, the oldest brother enlisted in the military when he was eighteen. After his two years of service, he moved in with his girlfriend's family. They got married a year after that and continued living with his wife's relatives. They could not afford a place of their own.

The other four brothers were living at home.

Alejandro, though he tried, never completed high school. He enrolled in a drama school and started going out to nightclubs with his friends.

Roberto and Jaime dropped out of elementary school. They helped their father build a couple of apartments in the empty lot next to the main house. Later, they decided to join the military service together.

Juan Carlos, the youngest, was a soul without an

aim. He dropped out of school before any of his other brothers did. He had odd jobs, but nothing lasted for very long. He died in a motorcycle accident when he was twenty-one.

"They need me, my son. They need me more than you do," Ana finally said to Pedro.

"You have always been able to take care of yourself, and even helped me with them," she said as she hugged and kissed him, then rose to go back to the kitchen to finish preparing dinner.

After she left, Pedro said silently, "I do need you, Mom. I need you just as much as they do. I'm feeling all alone here, and I don't know what to do. Now, I need to find a new place to live once again."

He covered his face and cried.

The following afternoon before going back to his aunt's house, Pedro decided to take a walk.

His mother, who saw him before reaching the door, asked him teasingly, "Are you going to visit and talk to your imaginary friend? What was his name?"

"I just need some fresh air, Mom," he told her, avoiding his mother's question.

Pedro walked to where he used to visit with Don Gregorio. There was nothing there, just an empty space. As he looked around, he felt a profound sense of sadness and an indescribable pain in the middle of his chest.

Pedro lay down in the fetal position to feel the pain and stay with it for a while. Later, with his hands on his chest, gazing up to the sky, he watched the clouds moving. As the clouds moved, they uncovered a magnificent blue sky, only for him to see that magnificence being covered again by new clouds.

Framed by the big old trees, the sky looked almost like a circle.

"You seemed so real to me when I was a kid. Your words used to comfort and guide me when I needed it. I always felt a sense of peace and joy in your presence.

"Where did you go? Where are you now? Why did you leave me? I need you.

"Please talk to me. Let me know that I'm not alone, that you are there somewhere watching over me. I need help, please, please.

"I don't know what to do. I have to move once again, and I don't know where to go. There is no way I can live with my folks. I need to move forward.

"Please help me and guide me. I'm completely lost and I need to find my way," he said, continuing to look up at the blue sky. Tears rolling down his cheeks, Pedro found himself talking to Don Gregorio, as he did when he was a little boy.

Suddenly, he felt very tired. He could hardly keep his eyes open, and giving into that feeling, he fell asleep.

Immediately asleep, he started having a dream. He was walking without knowing where he was going. A deep fog prevented him from seeing clearly.

At a distance, he saw a dim light and walked towards it. As he approached, he realized that it was Don Gregorio's house.

He opened the door and walked in without even knocking.

Don Gregorio was in bed and looked very sick. Pedro rushed to the wooden bed and got on his knees to get closer to the old man.

"Oh my God, what's wrong with you?" Pedro cried.

"There is absolutely nothing wrong with me, just as there is nothing wrong with your family, Pedro. You have to stop judging and telling them what to do. They don't want the same things you do. They have their own lives to live, and you ought to respect and trust that.

"Love, trust and respect are not things that you get from people, Pedro. That's something that you give, and it comes back to you. But, never give it to expect it back in return.

"Trusting and respecting people and situations just as they are is love, and love, *love is the greatest force in this universe.*

"Your biggest lesson is learning to be around the flame without getting burned.

"We all don't want the same things, and that's the beauty of it all.

"Your mother has her own path and journey to travel.

"If you ask for tea, but water is all that is offered, then enjoy the water.

"If you find yourself in a situation you don't like, then change it. You have the power and the ability to do that. But remember that you are only an instrument of that power."

"All I want is the best for them," Pedro said, sobbing.

"Then do what is best for you. That's the only way you can do what is best for them. Don't try to change them.

"You are the only one you will ever be able to change.

"You are responsible for your own life, and they are responsible for theirs," Don Gregorio said in a weak voice.

With tears in his eyes Pedro begged him, "Please

don't leave me. I'm afraid. I'm very afraid, and I don't know what to do now."

"There is no separation, there is no separation, there is no separation," Pedro heard an echo in his head, as he woke up crying and saying, "please don't leave me, please don't leave me."

At this point, Pedro knew that he had to make the seemingly impossible possible.

. . .

Pedro decided to apply to go to school in the United States. Getting his passport took a little while, but getting all the required papers, applications and visa was the biggest challenge.

Pedro didn't know if it all would go through, but he had to try it.

His immediate family only found out about his leaving a week prior to his departure. He was afraid to tell them, in case something went wrong at the last minute. He wanted to make sure that everything was arranged before he said anything.

When he finally told them, none of his relatives believed him.

They knew that Pedro didn't know anyone in the United States, and that he neither spoke the language, nor had the means and finances to support himself there.

His father, who seriously doubted it, asked him, "Pedro, how would you even ask for food?"

Pedro answered, "I know a little bit of English."

The fact was that Pedro didn't speak the language at all. He had taken some English classes, but not enough to know the language.

He had been accepted into what was called English as a Second Language at Centenary College in Shreveport, Louisiana. He used his savings from his work as a government clerk to pay the initial tuition, and bought the plane ticket with his severance pay.

Following his arrival in the United States, he had three months of intensive English classes at Centenary. Then, he enrolled as a regular college student. He worked as a busboy and dishwasher in a restaurant during the week, and mowed lawns on the weekends.

While attending college in Louisiana, Pedro met his first boyfriend, Andy. He and Andy later decided to move to Chicago.

For Pedro, this offered the opportunity of more affordable education, and for Andy, graduate school. For the two of them, it was the chance to live together. Pedro was very much in love with Andy.

Andy had a lot of internal conflicts concerning his religious upbringing, beliefs and sexual orientation. He later left Pedro, and moved back to Louisiana.

Pedro, all alone and heartbroken, stayed in Chicago, and continued attending the university to finish his bachelor's degree—the impossible dream he had when he was a little boy.

TIME
There is a time
There is a time for laughing
There is a time for crying
There is a time for joy
There is time for sorrow
There is a time
There is a time…

CHAPTER 5

NOTHING IN LIFE IS PERMANENT

All of the graduates gathered with their families before lining up for the graduation ceremony.

Pedro noticed one of the graduates having trouble adjusting his graduation gown, so he offered to help.

"I've seen you around campus, but we never spoke. My name is Pedro," he said, extending his hand.

"Oh, yes! My name is Luis. I wanted to say hi, but you always seemed to be rushing out of school," he said, as he shook Pedro's hand.

Pedro looked around and said to Luis, "I guess we should congratulate each other. It seems like we are the only graduates without family here."

Luis came closer to Pedro and gave him a strong hug and told him, "Congratulations!" At that moment, "Pomp and Circumstance" started playing and Pedro got a little emotional. He tried to hide it from Luis, but tears just streamed down his cheeks.

"I'm sorry, I didn't think this was going to affect me this much," Pedro said.

"Please don't worry," Luis told him. He came closer to Pedro and gently wiped, with his thumb, a tear running down Pedro's face.

Everyone lined up, and all graduates were called by name. Pedro was impressed by how well his name was pronounced.

At the end of the ceremony, as Pedro was leaving, he heard someone calling his name. He turned and saw Luis rushing towards him.

"I was wondering if you were going to the reception?" Luis asked him.

"No, I have some people waiting for me."

"Would you like to go out for dinner sometime?"

"Sorry Luis, I have a partner, and I'm committed to him."

Disappointed, Luis told him, "No worries, I totally understand."

Luis turned to follow the crowd to the reception, and to Pedro's surprise, he felt his heart wrench, as he watched Luis walking away from him.

'I have a partner for God's sake. Why am I feeling this way about someone else?' he thought to himself.

His partner John and a couple of his partner's friends caught up with Pedro in the hall, as he was already walking towards the parking lot.

"Who was that?" John asked him.

"Someone I knew here at school."

"Wow, he's handsome!" one of his partner's friends said.

"Are you ready to go?" John asked.

"Yes, I am!"

Pedro walked ahead of the three of them.

"Is there anything wrong?" John asked him, when they got to the car.

"No, I just want to go." They got in the car and drove to a restaurant where they were meeting a few other friends.

Pedro was still feeling the emotions the graduation evoked as well as the crush Luis sparked in him with his gentleness and understanding.

Two years before graduation, Pedro had been diagnosed with the HIV virus. It was the next challenge in Pedro's life.

After graduation, Pedro got a job at one of the city colleges. Sometime after that, he also started practicing yoga with an HIV group.

One evening, the yoga instructor invited a Buddhist nun to join them. The nun gave a talk on the subjects of impermanence and attachment. She talked about how attachments and wanting things to remain the same will cause us suffering.

"Nothing in life is permanent. Everything is in a constant change," the nun told the group at the end.

These two subjects fascinated Pedro, and they made so much sense to him. It reminded him of the waves, he watched as a child, constantly moving and changing, nothing ever staying the same. He decided to investigate more about Buddhism and meditation.

Pedro began regularly attending a meditation service on Sunday mornings. The meditation service consisted of sitting meditation, chanting and a short Dharma talk by the Zen priest. Pedro found it to be the only place where by just sitting he felt whole, and that there was nothing particularly wrong with him. For that brief hour, it didn't matter what was going on in his outside world, and his HIV status. He was just fine.

The Zen priest would usually say, at the beginning of the sitting:

"Sit like a mountain. Wind may blow, rain may fall, sun may shine, mountain sits still."

He would close the phrase by saying:

"Sitting takes care of you."

Pedro didn't understand how sitting could do that. But, the fact was that practicing always gave him that sense of trust and peace that he did not find anywhere else. The media, his friends and even his own partner only spoke of those who were sick and dying.

Pedro told his partner that he did not want to hear any more about people dying or sick. He only wanted to hear about those who were living, and living well, because that was what he was intending to do.

Pedro's interest in meditation and learning more about other cultures and religions threatened his partner. His partner didn't like beliefs and practices different from his own.

John told Pedro, "What do you want to do, go around with a bowl asking for food? All those cultures are dead poor. Is that what you want for your life?"

Pedro responded by asking him, "Have you ever thought that they may have the wisdom and strength of being that poor and yet still being happy?

"Maybe their wealth is not related to money, but rather peace and joy in their hearts, and that's what I want.

"Having joy in one's heart, no matter what's going on in the outside, is something that cannot be bought by all the wealth in this world."

After eight years, Pedro's relationship with John ended.

John asked Pedro to move out, but never thought that Pedro would actually leave given his circumstances.

Pedro found himself in poor health with no partner, no place to go, no family, and no job. He had just been laid off from a company where he was working as an accountant. He agreed to move by the end of that month.

Pedro knew that it was time to end the relationship and move on. This was a difficult time for him, and his partner knew it.

Though painful and scary, Pedro thought that being asked to move was the best gift. It gave him the courage to do the right thing.

Pedro knew that staying in that relationship was going to kill him faster than the HIV virus. His partner's fears, insecurities, narrow- mindedness and his possessiveness were too much to handle. Pedro already had enough trying to cope with his own condition.

Most gatherings and social events were with his partner's friends. Pedro's friends were rarely included. His partner was never happy when Pedro spent time with some of his friends.

Pedro really didn't feel fully included in the relationship. This was a very hard and sad realization, but one that he needed to honestly face.

Pedro thought, 'If I were to stay in the house, I would have food and a place to live to save and protect my physical body. But, I would be slowly crushing my spirit.'

Pedro chose to care for his spirit rather than his physical safety. He had already made up his mind to go to a homeless shelter if he could not find a place to live by the end of that month. He knew that this would potentially expose him to a lot of infections, but it was a risk he was willing to take.

Pedro closed his eyes and thought:

'The spirit can save the physical body, but the body can never save the spirit, and this is only a body. This is what's best for the whole. Don't be afraid. Trust that everything is unfolding perfectly.'

In a way, it was as if his old friend, Don Gregorio, were speaking to him.

He knew that the spirit did not need saving and would never die, only the body does. This was the thought that helped him to go through, face and trust what was to come with the ending of the relationship.

Though Pedro loved his partner, it was no longer a healthy situation for either one of them.

His partner told Pedro that he would appreciate it if he wouldn't ask for help from any of their common friends. Pedro was not even thinking of asking for help from any of his own personal friends. He understood that this was something he needed to face and come to terms with on his own.

They really were no longer a couple. His partner was HIV negative, and very afraid of the HIV issue.

Pedro was already HIV positive when they met, but did not find out until later. Fortunately, his partner never contracted the virus.

The weekend before he was supposed to move, Pedro heard a friend talking about someone looking for a roommate.

Pedro contacted that person and got the room. He was very grateful to have found a place.

The roommate was gracious enough to allow Pedro to have the room and move in, even without a job. Pedro promised his roommate that he would pay the security deposit, as soon as he got a new job.

Pedro was so thankful. Once alone, he got on his knees and kissed the floor of his new bedroom.

"Thank you, thank you, thank you," he said, as he kneeled and bowed his head to the floor with his hands in a prayer position.

Soon after that, he found another accounting position, and was able to pay the amount owed for the security deposit to his new roommate.

After some time had passed, Pedro and his ex-partner became very close and good friends. Pedro felt, at that time, that John was the only real family he had in the city.

John told Pedro in birthday cards, postcards, letters and e-mails the things Pedro would have loved to hear while they were together.

HEAVEN AND EARTH
There is heaven,
There is earth.
They come together,
And there is you.

CHAPTER 6

STAYING WITH THE QUESTION

After Pedro moved to his new place, he continued attending the Sunday morning meditation.

One Sunday morning, during the brief Dharma talk after the sitting, the Zen priest stopped right in front of Pedro. He said to Pedro, in his heavy Japanese accent, "I saw you on TV last week. Now, I know you have HIV."

Pedro had given an interview for "World AIDS Day" during the evening news the week before.

"I say to you," the priest spoke directly to Pedro:

"Things are not what they seem; nor are they otherwise.

"Don't be fooled by your thoughts. Whatever

situation you are in is truly precious. Not a matter of good or bad, right or wrong, win or lose, beneficial or not beneficial. But so it is.

"We're all in the process of changing, becoming and moving on," he said.

He took one of the chant booklets from a pew, opened it and read out loud from the Bodhisattva's vow:

"When I, a student of Dharma,
Look at the real form of the universe,
All is the never-failing manifestation
Of the mysterious truth of Tathagata.
In any event, in any moment, and in any place,
None can be other than the marvelous revelation
Of its glorious light…"

He closed the chanting book and said, "This is my sharing for today." He bowed to the group and the group bowed back to him.

That morning after meditation, Pedro decided to go for a walk by the park. It was a sunny and warm winter day.

He sat on a bench by a pond. The edge of the

pond was frozen, but rapidly melting due to the warm weather.

A young woman, not too far from where Pedro was sitting, was standing and looking out at the water.

Pedro thought of the statement that the Zen priest had told him earlier, 'Things are not what they seem; nor are they otherwise.'

Pedro didn't quite understand the significance of that statement. But part of him completely connected with it. Somehow, he perceived the meaning without really understanding it. He couldn't put it into words. He said it out loud without realizing it, "Things are not what they seem; nor are they otherwise."

The woman standing by the railing must have heard him. She turned to him and said, "There's no one answer for life."

Surprised that the woman even spoke to him, Pedro responded by saying, "Pardon me?"

"We have no control over life. Life is just happening as it does. Once you think that you have an answer for it, that's exactly when you miss it. And that which is supposedly missed is not separate from life. Trying to understand this is not facing life, but not facing it is also part of life.

"It's like the personal looking for the impersonal, when the impersonal lies at the heart of the personal.

"The projection is never separate from the projector.

"This does not mean not to ask the question.

"Maybe just staying with the question is enough. Who knows?" She said, as she gently smiled at him.

"It's a gorgeous day, isn't it?" she asked him.

"Yeah," Pedro responded, almost in shock.

"Enjoy the rest of your day," she said, as she walked away.

'What was that all about?' he thought.

"Hmm, maybe I just need to stay with the question," he said to himself and smiled.

Seconds later when he looked to see where the woman went, she was already gone.

NO-THING-NESS
(Beyond things)
One cannot understand matter, until one can grasp the concept that
it manifested from no-thing, and it evolved and changed through
its own thought. And this no-thing-ness is in fact everything;
therefore from this no-thing everything is possible and there are no
limitations.

CHAPTER 7

WHAT YOU THINK IS WHAT YOU GET

A friend invited Pedro to her church. She told him that a Zen priest was invited as a guest speaker.

As they walked into the party room of her church, Pedro saw that it was the same Zen priest from where he attended meditation.

'He really doesn't discriminate whom he shares his wisdom with,' Pedro thought, as he smiled.

Pedro's friend asked him, "What are you smiling about?"

"I know him. He is the Buddhist minister where I go for meditation on Sunday mornings.

"Let's sit in the back," Pedro suggested to his friend.

After the Zen priest was introduced, he started by saying:

"You are the only one with your life, and when you walk in the rain you get wet."

Pedro suspected that statement already confused most people. Also the strong Japanese accent made it sound like there was mystery behind the words.

"Instead of being caught by a happening, rather see it, face it, overcome it and learn from it," he said, as he got closer to one of the people sitting in the front row. He looked at the person right in the eyes, as he had always done to those at the dharma talks on Sundays.

Then, he raised his gaze to see the whole group and said, "What you think is what you get.

"With our practice we want to break through simply acquiring knowledge; we want to break through preconceived ideas of trying to fix something. Then a new vision or way of living our lives will be born."

Pedro felt like he was talking to him, though he had not seen him yet.

"The worst enemy in our life is to believe that 'I am absolutely right.' The middle way path is not one-sided. It's not extremely negative or extremely positive. Rather, both sides are unified and harmonized.

"The truth manifests itself into life." As he said that, he finally noticed Pedro in the back of the room. He slightly nodded to him in a form of recognition.

He had always looked at Pedro with this intensity, as if he had just seen a long lost friend. This sometimes made Pedro feel a little bit uneasy.

"When I was in high school, like other teenagers," he continued, "I had the desire to be attractive and smart. I blamed my mother that I wasn't as attractive and smart as I wanted to be.

"I complained to her, *You should have given me more brains! Plus I need longer legs. I want to be taller than I am. Why did you make me like this?*

"My mother responded, *When I was pregnant with you, I hoped and prayed to have an attractive, smart son.... But you came out!*"

Everybody laughed.

The Zen priest never held back to show his own humanity. He let everyone know that he was not different.

"I still remember my mother responding to me in this manner. It made me look at myself as I was, not as I wanted to be. I realized I had such wants, such attachments.... But so did my mother!

"Universal truth is manifested right in front of you."

The Zen priest was never about converting people into Buddhists, but to teach universal truth. He knew that universal truth did not belong to any particular religion or tradition.

Pedro saw how this could get him into trouble with some of his temple members with a very strong Buddhist identification.

"We don't like the suffering in our lives," the priest went on to say.

"We say that is bad, that it causes us a lot of pain and trouble. Yet it helps us, like the dirty bottom of a pond that helps the lotus flower to go beyond the dirt and become beautiful; like cow shit."

People laughed again as he said that.

He waited until people stopped laughing. Then he continued, "It smells and looks bad to us, and yet helps us to produce a beautiful garden that we enjoy.

"Be like a mirror. It will reflect you as you are, but when you move away from it, the mirror becomes clear. It will reflect dog shit, but the mirror doesn't smell."

This time the people broke down into a continuous laughter. He definitely never took himself too seriously.

The laughter was triggered also by the fact that people never expected a priest to talk like that.

People felt shocked, and yet refreshed and more relaxed at the same time.

He tried to always break through the seriousness that most people took their lives to be.

Once people stopped laughing, he continued, "I think our life is like this. In order to see the vast, limitless, endless blue sky of our true nature, we have to break through the gray clouds that are in our lives."

Pedro knew that to the priest, taking ourselves too seriously was one of those clouds.

"You have to laugh," the priest would often say.

Most of the time one would see him smiling or laughing. So, he did practice that in his life.

He continued, "As we live our lives, we need to go through and through and through!

"The true nature of our life is this huge blue sky, but we don't see it. We spend lots of time worrying about the clouds instead of going through them. I think we can use our worries and cares to help us break through to the blue sky of our true nature.

"There is no doubt about it; the blue sky is always there. If you look up when the sky is completely filled with dark clouds, you won't see the blue sky, but it is there. So go beyond the clouds and break through, break through. Go through and through and through, and you will enjoy the blue sky!"

As he finished his talk, he thanked and bowed to the group. He stayed to answer people's questions.

Pedro decided to leave. There were a lot of people wanting to talk to him. Pedro really never had anything to ask him or tell him for that matter. Their communication was mostly silent.

They saw each other before Pedro left, and said hello and goodbye at the same time without a word.

WHAT WE CALL TROUBLE
All challenges conceal within the seed of
Our own well-being, growth and development.
But, as with all things, one needs to care and
Nurture it for that seed to bear fruit.
If we resent or avoid our
Challenges, we miss
That opportunity.

CHAPTER 8

THE STORY WILL ALWAYS KEEP YOU IN THE HOUSE OF FEAR

During the springtime, Pedro decided to go to the Work and Practice Period Program at a Zen Monastery in California, where he met Aleah.

The everyday work, the three times daily sitting, as well as the communal life were all considered part of the practice at the monastery.

The monastery was open to visitors during this period.

Aleah and Pedro worked together cleaning the guests' cabins. They became very good friends while working and practicing together.

During one of the work period breaks, Pedro complained to Aleah about the crew leader:

"He told me not to clean cabin twenty and later asked me if I had it ready.

"How am I supposed to have it ready, when he told me to take it off my list?" Pedro accused the crew leader.

Aleah kindly said to Pedro, "Well Pedro, there are only two houses one could go; the house of fear or the house of love.

"Being upset is a valid response and it may be needed for the process of moving from one house to the other.

"Sometimes seeing your challenges as a blessing or a gate for growth, rather than as a curse or problem can shift your mind almost immediately."

"How does this concept of the house of fear and the house of love work?"

"Well, in the house of fear, one can experience anger. On the other hand, in the house of love, one can experience peace and joy.

"You will always be at a higher frequency in the house of love because you would be going with the flow of life rather than against it. Exercise the power of nonresistance to "what is".

"Anything you resist persists and anything you fight against you strengthen."

"But Aleah, he does this to me all the time. This really makes me mad. Is this some kind of test he's putting me through?

"Does he do that to you?" Pedro asked Aleah very angrily.

"No, but he's kind of goofy," she said smiling.

She continued, "No matter how justifiable, the story will always keep you in the house of fear. Drop the story and stay with the feelings."

"I just wish he wouldn't do that," Pedro said.

"You're wishing for things to be different from what they are at this moment.

"So, would you rather be happy or would you rather be right, sometimes it's just as simple as that. Don't fight it, go through it, and let the process flow and stop wanting it to be different."

"Aleah, what am I supposed to do?"

"Don't ask for the situation to change, but for the situation to change you. Then, the situation might change, as a by-product. But don't be attached to anything.

"You have no control over what he does, but what you do. If you shoot the messenger you will miss the message.

"Blaming him for his actions will not help you. Bringing it back to you may be a better choice."

"Is this some kind of process that I need to go through?"

"Yes, and the process is simple," she said.

"Cradle it in the arms of love. Witness whatever feelings, emotions and thoughts arising from your consciousness without identifying with them or judging them. Just let each arise, observe it, with no resistance, accept it, thank it and let it go."

"How would this help?" he asked her, frustrated.

"As you do that, you'll come to a point where your mind will see the futility of those thoughts and settle into its true nature. Then, you will realize the changing nature and insubstantiality of all things.

"When we confront something that we don't like, one can be assured it's one of our own shadows in need of integration. It's likely that he's reflecting something back for you to see, so this situation may be giving you the opportunity for that to be brought up. Life to us is a mystery, but we're that mystery.

"There is always a hidden message in all that happens to us; you have to be open to it," she said.

"Aleah, at this moment, I don't want to be integrated or get any messages, especially from him. I don't like him," Pedro said to her and they both laughed.

Pedro knew that Aleah was right.

But, he kept finding himself in the same hole.

Pedro had no problem understanding what Aleah was saying, but putting it into practice was never easy.

Later, as they walked to the mid-day sitting, Aleah said to him, "There are two things a person can do. A person can either separate or integrate. Separation or identification is ego, and it limits you to the small or limited mind. Integration or unification is oneness, and it connects you to the big or universal mind.

"Every time you justify or defend Pedro, you separate and connect to the limited mind.

"Allowing it all to be and go through it unifies you.

"But at the same time, no matter what, the infinite and the finite are one. This is the paradox of life," she said, as they got closer to the Zendo for the midday sitting.

The practice of non-judgment, gratitude and compassion had always helped Pedro. Being as open as possible to all people and situations had always brought a sense of peace to him, even with those situations and people he did not like or agree with.

One of the practices Pedro liked to use when he disagreed with or disliked someone—or even with people who had hurt him—was to repeat over and over again, as a mantra in his head, "May she or he be happy, may she or he be peaceful, may she or he be joyful."

He also wished the same thing for himself.

This practice always helped him to move from the house of fear into the house of love, or break the gap of the perceived separation and integrate or unify, as his friend Aleah had put it.

Pedro decided to go to the evening talk that night. It was a guest speaker from Russia.

She started by saying, "Wanting things to be different from what they are will always cause us suffering."

Pedro almost chuckled, when he heard her say that.

"But, even our own suffering can be experienced as a gift, if we only give ourselves that opportunity. The experience itself is the gift from beyond," she continued.

"You have to stay in close contact with the energy that arises—like fear, grief, or anger. Feel them in your body as they arise from your own experiences at every opportunity. Do not try to change anything, just observe what is happening and be present with that energy in your body.

"As you maintain and abide in that energy and integrate it into your life experiences in that way, over and over again, it helps you connect.

"You can also focus on your breath to keep this presence and then you may return to the physical sensations in your body.

"It's not so much about what's going on outside, as it is to what's going on inside. At the same time, outside and inside are not separate.

"In meditation, we do not try to change anything in the outer world. Instead, we observe, connect and rest in that connection. By doing not doing, transformation appears to happen in our sensorial and perceived world.

"In the world of forms, we're bound by the law of matter and ruled by the five senses. But in the space of stillness, silence and presence, everything is possible and there is no limitation.

"We connect in meditation with the formless part of ourselves, moving more from human to being and from being to nonbeing. All things are born from being, but being is born from nonbeing, and they are not separate. It's more like a projector and its projection.

"All types of mental activity and identification with the projection create confusion and separate us from who we are.

"We're not what we think, but thoughts arise from and are part of THAT. We're not our experience, but our experiences are born from THAT. There's nothing pure or impure in THAT. Everything is equal and born from THAT.

"THAT can never be known, only "its" reflection in and as all forms. The reflection is awareness. THAT is prior to awareness or consciousness.

"THAT can only be expressed as a paradox, like emptiness is full. It's nothing that the mind can perceive or conceive as a thing, and there is no essential "THAT". Everything is ever changing and radically interconnected.

"As we live in this world of relative separateness, we're bound by the fruit of our own actions. This fruit may be sweet or sour according to the seed that was planted. This all begins with a thought in the world of forms."

Then, she closed by saying:

"It's like going with the same force and direction that the river is already going. Steering the boat down the middle without taking refuge on either bank and finding resting islands along the way.

"We make a choice of responding or reacting at every step of the journey.

"It's knowing what to refrain from and what to cultivate. The choice is ours.

"Ultimately, it's integrating with that force and developing the trust, the confidence and the faith to let go and let be no matter what. Sometimes that means taking refuge on one of the riverbanks, and seeing the perfection in all things.

"Allow and become that primordial space that cannot be punctured by an arrow, then that which is perceived as real by the senses may just become an illusion."

The evening speaker practically repeated what Aleah had already told him earlier.

Pedro knew that Aleah was one of those resting islands.

I AM
I am nothing, but yet I am everything.
I am nowhere, but yet I am everywhere.

CHAPTER 9

LOVE ALLOWS EVERYTHING, AND DOESN'T PUSH ANYTHING AWAY

After returning from California, Pedro started suffering from chronic bronchitis. He had a high viral load and very low T-cell count. He was later diagnosed with full-blown AIDS and had several bad cases of pneumonia. He also started having some memory problems and chronic fatigue.

To prevent pneumonia, he started taking Bactrum. He was not able to tolerate the drug and it caused a rash all over his body. He became extremely sick and was hardly able to move. He had body aches all over, night sweats, fevers and no energy.

He was hospitalized a few times during these illnesses. The closest hospital to his house was Saint Joseph's Catholic Hospital. On one occasion, Pedro was so ill that the doctors thought that he might not pull through. A nurse asked Pedro, if he would like a chaplain or a priest to come visit him, and Pedro agreed.

Later that afternoon, a Catholic priest came to visit.

"Hello Mr. Rodriguez, my name is Father Rodney. How are you doing today?" the priest asked.

"I'm doing much better now that you are here," Pedro responded with a smile.

"I noticed that you don't have a denomination on your chart," he said.

"I don't have one. But, I was raised Catholic," Pedro told the priest.

"So, when did you walk away from the Catholic Church?" Father Rodney asked.

"I didn't. I just expanded it, Father," he responded.

Pedro knew that Father Rodney was a little confused, so he tried to explain it. "Father, it's just like an orchard. In this orchard there are many different types of trees and fruits, and I see the beauty and richness in all of them. I decided not to limit myself to just one, but rather be nurtured by all of them. That's what I mean by expanding it.

I'll always be somewhat Catholic because of my Catholic mother, but with a broader point of view. Now, I respect, appreciate and learn from all religions and traditions."

Father Rodney asked him, "Is it okay if I pray for you?"

Pedro responded by saying, "Please do. I know how powerful a prayer can be, especially when it comes from the heart."

Later, after Father Rodney left, the nurse came to give Pedro some morphine to help him with the pain. She told him that it would also help him relax.

Pedro was in the isolation room at the hospital. He was wearing one of those hospital gowns that he never knew what was the right way to put it on.

He saw his mother sitting on the right side of his bed holding his hand.

"Mom, how did you get here?" he asked her.

"I missed you so much, and I wanted to come to see you, my son," his mother answered.

He really didn't know if he was awake, dreaming, or if it was the effect of the morphine the nurse had just given him through the I.V.

"We all know that in your heart, you always had good intentions, and you only wanted what was best for us," his mother said.

"But I had it all wrong, Mom. I just didn't know," he responded.

"You were just confused, my son. You thought that we ought to want the same things that you did," his mother tried to console him.

"We all have our own journey to travel, and so did you, my son. Life and your own journey took you away from us," his mother continued.

At that moment, Pedro remembered what his friend Bernardo had told him. Bernardo had said to Pedro that he no longer belonged there. He needed to leave, to be on his own, to move forward, and to open a new path to pursue his goals and dreams.

Pedro felt rejected when some of his relatives directly or indirectly asked him to move. At the same time, they had just done what they thought was the right thing to do. As painful as it was, that did push him to move forward.

Suddenly, all the hurt he had held inside from feeling unwanted completely disappeared.

Then, he realized that he was the one who needed to ask for forgiveness.

"Forgive me, please forgive me, please forgive me," he begged his mother, as tears poured down the sides of his face.

"My dearest son, it's all about forgiving the unforgivable and embracing the unembraceable," his mother replied with the same kindness and love that she had always shown him.

"The key to the kingdom of God is love. Love allows everything, and doesn't push anything away. Be as close to love as you can, and please, please continue on, my son," his mother said, as she vanished.

He did not want to let go of his mother's hand. As he finally did, he woke up crying and saying, "I love you, Mom. I love you, Mom."

It had all been a dream.

Pedro believed that the end of his road was near. He felt a profound sense of sadness to see it all end, here and now.

He remembered what his mother had told him in the dream, 'love allows everything and doesn't push anything away.'

He decided to allow the sadness and let it be. He felt the sadness take over him. He offered no resistance. He stayed with that feeling. He allowed himself to be completely taken and present with the sadness. As he did this, he noticed something shifting within. It was like crossing over from sadness to joy. He realized that allowing it to be was the bridge.

The nurse came into the room to give him his medication. He asked her for a pen. He took a piece of paper from the drawer and wrote:

In the midst of my own sadness, I discovered my

own joy.

As he finished putting down that thought, he heard a voice say, "You're going to be alright."

"Did you hear that?" Pedro asked the nurse.

"Hear what?" she asked.

"The voice," he told her.

"What voice? There is only you and me in the room, Mr. Rodriguez."

It was clear to Pedro that the nurse really didn't hear what he heard.

"Did I imagine it or did I hear it," Pedro questioned himself. He was not sure.

THE UNIVERSE
This universe:
When you respect it,
You are in paradise.
When you accept it,
You are in paradise.
When you follow the perfection of its flow,
You are in paradise.
And, when you become one with it,
You are paradise.

CHAPTER 10

I HAVE LEARNED TO RESPECT AND ACCEPT THE THINGS THAT I CANNOT CHANGE

The next day, after hearing the voice, the doctor came to see Pedro. The doctor told him that they were going to start him on a new class of drugs called protease inhibitors along with AZT.

"Studies have shown that this new class of drugs dramatically reduces the viral load," the doctor informed him.

After a couple of months, Pedro started to see the

results of what the doctor had predicted. Although there were several side effects to the new drugs, slowly they did start to lower his viral load. However, his T-cells remained dangerously low.

Pedro was able to live with the side effects, and the low T-cell count. He was looking forward to getting better.

Due to the hard winters in Chicago and the concern of pneumonia, Pedro thought about moving to Hawaii. A close friend reminded him that he had a longer journey to travel than moving to Hawaii. Pedro needed to tell his family about who he was and what he had.

Pedro decided to create a video to send to his family. He asked a few of his friends to help him with this project. His immigration status at that time prevented him from returning to his home country.

Pedro sent a letter along with the video to his family:

My dear family,

There are two things in my life that I want to

share with you. They represent only a small part of who I am, and it is my wish that you won't see them as something to hide or to feel ashamed of.

Through my life experiences I have learned to respect and accept the things that I cannot change, and to realize that nothing happens accidentally. Everything has its reason to be.

My sexual orientation is that of the same sex. Here in the United States we use the word "gay." It's very important for me not to deny my sexuality, because if we believe in the perfect creation of God but yet deny who we are, then we are denying the perfection of that creation.

I want you to know that I'm the same person who you have known and loved for 35 years. I hope my sexual orientation won't change that love.

To question, 'Why is a person homosexual?' is like questioning, 'Why is a person heterosexual?' or 'Why do trees have leaves?' or 'Why do the oceans have salt water and the rivers fresh water?' There are things in life that cannot be explained. They just simply are.

Our world is created based on our differences,

and we all have the capacity to accept them, respect them, and appreciate them, if we only give ourselves that opportunity. Our differences are a strength and not a weakness.

The second thing I wanted to share with you is that I was diagnosed with the AIDS virus in 1987. I remember during that year telling myself, although I didn't believe it, 'Something good is going to come out of this situation.'

Today, in 1995, I can say that having AIDS has given me the opportunity to learn and give the best of me, to enjoy and appreciate life for what it is, and not to resent it for what it's not.

This disease has helped me to understand that there is a part of me that is free of all disease that nobody can touch and nobody can break—my spiritual self.

This world we live in is a perfect creation, and every single human being is part of this creation. If we feel ashamed of who we are and what we have, then we are denying the perfection of this creation.

It is very important to be honest with one's self

and be like an open book in which everyone who wants to look and learn can do so. Denying or hiding limits us, and it denies us that sense of freedom that we all desire.

We all have the capacity to achieve whatever we want in our lives and to create our own reality according to our own decisions.

Patience is a virtue, and I have learned to take one step at a time.

I want you to know that sometimes I feel like the happiest man on earth. I am in good health; I have good friends, and all the necessary energy to work.

All I want is that the love and respect you have always felt for me will not change, and that you will feel as proud of me today as you did yesterday.

With all my love and respect,

Pedro.

Marcos, Pedro's eldest brother, who viewed the video and read the letter, decided not to show it to the rest of the family.

Since their father had just recently passed away, Marcos told Pedro that the family was not ready for anything like that.

Pedro, feeling the responsibility to inform his family about his HIV status, agreed to edit out the part that talked about his sexual orientation.

Though his brother did not tell him, Pedro knew this was the major problem Marcos had in sharing the information. Then, after editing the sexual orientation part out, his brother agreed to share it with the rest of the family.

Pedro had a conversation with his mother over the phone prior to her viewing or reading the edited version of the video and letter.

After Pedro told his mother the content of the video and letter, his mother responded to Pedro by saying, "If it is a miracle that we need, then that's what we'll ask for my dearest son."

His mother's kind words gave Pedro a great sense of peace, and lifted a heavy burden from his heart. That was all Pedro needed to hear.

TALKING TO THE LAKE
I asked the lake this morning how I could be as strong and powerful as it was, and to give so much. So many creatures live in you. People have contaminated your waters and taken from your land, and you still keep on giving. The lake said, "Pedro, it's the giving that makes me strong. It's the giving that makes me powerful. It's the giving that gives me the reason to keep on living." Now I want the lake to live inside of me. Thank you my friend, for teaching and helping
me to find so much peace within me.

CHAPTER 11

GO BEYOND

A few years later Pedro visited Israel to attend a Science and Spirituality conference, and there he met James, a Christian and a physicist.

At the end of the conference, Pedro and James decided to visit the Mosque at Temple Mount, the Dome of the Rock.

After visiting the Mosque, they went for a walk to the West Wall. They later sat in a park and talked. James was an older, wise and funny man. He always made Pedro laugh.

While talking, Pedro asked him, "What would you say is the difference between reactive and proactive?"

"Well, even though people and situations in our lives affect our experiences, we have a choice to be reactive or proactive. We're reactive when we blame the outside world, people and situations. We're proactive when we look to learn something from those situations and people.

"In the space between stimulus and response lies our growth and transformation—the opportunity to make a correction, rather than to get ourselves more entangled by our reactions. It's like taking two steps back to be able to see the bigger picture, in order to move forward."

"So, this is the way to bring the practice into this world?"

"Precisely, with every single situation in our life, being proactive is not just taking the easy and the usual way out, but creating something new. It's embracing a situation or a person that appears to be working against you. It's doing for another that which you may not particularly like or enjoy. It's doing what's best for the whole, rather than for your benefit alone. This is true giving and sharing. Be *the cause* of something new, instead of *the effect* of your habitual reactions."

Pedro wished he had not been so reactive with his family, when he was younger. He now had a greater appreciation, love and respect for all of his relatives.

"I guess it's also about not regretting, right?" Pedro asked.

"Right, it's not about regretting the past or worrying about the future. *Trust what is* at that moment without reacting to the experience. Give up control and manipulation and all you're left with is the perfect flow of life. The flame is not there to burn you. The flame is there to awaken you."

Then, Pedro recalled what Don Gregorio had told him in the dream long ago:

'Your biggest lesson is learning how to be around the flame without getting burned.'

James later said, "We are all leaves from the same

tree, Pedro. We're all connected—you're me, and I'm you. My happiness is not independent from yours.

"Whenever we wish or cause harm to others, we do it to ourselves. Our own happiness lies in the happiness and joy that we give to others.

"It's like the ending of the Newtonian era from which we learned about the physical world and separateness, and the beginning of a new era of unification, as quantum physics tells us now.

"We have more scientific knowledge today than ever before, but we have not understood this knowledge in a way that awakens us."

"So, what does quantum physics say?"

"At a sub-atomic level, quantum physics tells us that it's all a unified field, which embodies all possibilities. You're one of those possibilities.

"In a more philosophical way, this oneness with the divine or to come together with God has been taught, and is one of the cornerstones of all the world's religions. Science is only now catching up.

"The separation is only a perception. That perception is just an interpretation of the brain through the senses, which creates that sense of separation."

"Man, I have to think about that one," Pedro smiled, and went on to ask, "What would you say reality is, then?"

"Reality is an interpretation of the perception of life by conditionings."

"But, we do see something out there. I see the trees. I see the cars. I see the people. I see you and see me."

"Yes, through the senses, one perceives and sees the other. But when you look deeply and truly into the source of life, there is no other. There is not that duality perceived by the senses of you and me or of a subject and object.

"It's like a world where there is no time and there is no space. It's all time and all space present together. There is no you and there is no me.

"It's like standing on a place where there is no ground."

"I cannot understand or even imagine a world without time and space or standing on a place where there is no ground," Pedro said and laughed out loud.

As he smiled, James said, "This cannot be understood by the mind my friend. But, you could start by imagining it.

"With the right effort and willingness, going beyond the senses is an evolutionary and a natural process for human beings' realization.

"All that you'll ever see is a footprint. You'll never see the real thing.

"I believe, that ultimately it's going beyond the senses, dropping and letting go of all these thoughts, beliefs and concepts and surrendering into 'what is'."

"What roles do science and spirituality play on what we perceive as real?" Pedro asked.

"Science and spirituality can be a bridge or a road map to go beyond that perception. The finger can only point to the moon; it's not the moon itself. If you get stuck on the finger, you'll never see the moon."

Pedro then inquired, "Is it like taking a taxi, if you don't get out of the taxi, you'll never experience the place where the taxi took you?"

"Correct, that's a good metaphor. Another one could be if you're too attached to the form, you'll never see the formless. Don't get the map confused with the territory. A dogma can be more of a limitation than liberation. You have to drop all of that at one point.

"We go from the simple to the complex. The only way to understand the complex is to go back to the simple."

"How do we do that?"

"Without judgment, become an observer of your body, thoughts, words and actions. In science, it's said that the process of observation affects that which has been observed."

"What are we changing with the observation?"

"We're not changing anything out there. It appears like something happens out of nothing actually happening, other than the observation.

The observation seems to affect what's been observed, and as a result the outer perception of what is called reality. There is a power in observation that cannot be explained."

Pedro pushed further, "Is it like training ourselves through observation not to react?"

"Perhaps, because nothing can ever be said for sure. Everything we say, the opposite could also be true. From where we stand, we can never see the whole elephant."

"So, would you say that by experiencing the branch one would know the roots?"

"You said it better and in even fewer words than I did." James smiled.

"Is it like meditation?" Pedro asked, since he had not heard James use that word.

"Sure, use your meditation as a tool to help you be the observer.

"Approach your meditation with the same great sense of love and respect, as we saw today the Muslims have praying to Allah."

Later James said, "Life will always give you the opportunity to practice with your own experiences."

"What other tools can we use?" inquired Pedro.

"We can also use the power of intention, gratitude and prayer. Always observe and question your intentions, be grateful for what you have, and pray for those who you perceive to be your aggressors or enemies. They're your teachers and angels sent from a concealed world or dimension to help you. Ask for guidance to help you be with the flow of life to follow the Tao.

"Give it all your attention, for what you're coming to know or to remember is nothing short of magnificent."

"What is the relationship between us and the magnificent, and also this thing that we call life, Dr. James?" Pedro asked him with a grin on his face.

"We're all expressions of that magnificence. But, we're not just that expression.

"It's not as if one becomes the light, as it is that

one starts developing the quality of the light to give. Therefore, as we develop that quality, one is not as affected by those situations in life.

"What would that be like?" Pedro asked.

"It's like going from *what can I get* to *what can I give*; at the same time that you're totally open to receive. It's like breathing, as you breathe in, you take in, as you breathe out, you give out. The two have to work together in complete and perfect harmony.

"It's a natural state of the creature to receive, but it's the quality of the creator to give. As we develop the quality of giving, we may realize similarity with the light.

"This entire creation is the light of the creator, just like the rays of light are of the sun, but the rays don't know that yet," James said and shrugged.

"What's needed for that to happen, Mr. Krishna?" Pedro asked him, remembering Arjuna always questioning Lord Krishna in the Bhagavad Gita.

"What's required is a large number of people, or a critical mass, to come to this realization. Then, all of creation would realize that what is perceived as separate or two, is in fact the same thing or one."

"Then, there would be peace in the world, right?" Pedro asked jokingly.

"You took the words out of my mouth," James responded and they both laughed.

"What about religions?" Pedro asked him.

"Religions are like lamps. The light is the same, but the shades are all different. If one believes his or her shade to be the one and only way, that will not only separate him or her from the other lamps, but also from the very own light that he or she proclaims."

James told Pedro, "Form is emptiness, and that emptiness, at the same time, is all forms, as the heart sutra states it. Treat everyone and everything as such."

"Love thy neighbor as thy self?"

"Correct!" James responded, happy to see that Pedro put those two together.

"But these are only pointers to that which has

neither beginning nor end, hence it cannot be grasped by the mind—the zero point as it's referred to in science. It's from where everything arises and to where everything falls back."

Again, for Pedro, a thought of his childhood came to mind:

'The wave and the ocean.'

"If there is no separation, what is the zero point then?" Pedro asked, as if he had him in a corner.

"I guess you could say the glue that connects all, but even that is incorrect because there is no glue."

"You mean because there is no time and there is no space?"

"My wife is an atheist, and she is as wrong and right as a believer, and I love her."

"So, we're talking about something that is not of this perceived world?" Pedro continued.

"It appears to be not of this world, as we perceive it. Anything we can say in this perceived world will always elude it. The mind, with all its words, is just not capable of describing it. "Don't know" is as close as you'll ever get, and even to say that is another form of identification or ego.

"It's just pure mystery to the thinking mind," James said, as he raised his eyebrows and grinned.

"So, tell me, what is ego then?" Pedro probed deeper.

"I guess, ego can be seen as the flame, where if you don't give it any more wood, the flame dies out, Mr. Arjuna."

"What is the wood that one puts into the fire?" Pedro pressed on.

"The constant reactivity to the situations in life. Now, I'm starting to sound like I know and practice this in my life. Don't let me fool you. I struggle with it as much as you do. Sometimes, I go through some waves of depression that I can hardly take myself out of."

Pedro always had one more last question. He asked him, as they were already on the way to the hotel, "What is the best approach one can take, Mr. Emptiness, or should I call you Mr. Zero

Point?"

"Well, a Kabbalist might say that when a situation arises, the first thing to recognize is that everything comes from the creator, or you may call it the light if that feels better. Second, notice your wanting to react, acknowledge it and let that go. Third, ask for help and allow for the light to come in, so you won't let the force of ego get the best of you. Last, do what needs to be done. Sometimes, there is nothing one needs to do my friend, but to *trust*."

Pedro remembered a prayer that came into his mind in a form of a poem long ago, when he didn't know what to do. He was afraid and he couldn't find an answer for his HIV status. All that was left was to pray and to trust:

'Please, give me the light to follow my path. And if I cannot have the light, please give me the trust to be in the dark.'

Finally James told him when they got to the hotel, "The process is already and always moving forward, like a river. It's all about how much you are willing to be with it. If one takes the invitation to flow along, one may experience synchronicity. If one doesn't flow along, and instead resists, tries to control, stop, change, or manipulate it, one will encounter suffering."

After getting to his room, Pedro decided to observe himself, as James had suggested. He took a shower, got dressed and laid on the bed to rest before meeting the group later for dinner.

He resisted the temptation to turn on the TV. He made a correction and instead, he reached out and grabbed the book of Rumi's poems that he had left on the nightstand. He read the next poem:

Come to the orchard in Spring.
There is light and wine,
And sweethearts in the pomegranate flowers.
If you do not come, these do not matter.
If you do come, these do not matter.

"I must be in some kind of synchronized flow," he said to himself and laughed.

He closed the book, put it back on the nightstand and continued to observe. He took a deep breath in and let it out. He did that once more, and closed his eyes.

He resumed to a relaxed and normal breathing. He became aware of the breath by noticing each inhalation and each exhalation, and the rising and falling of the chest and abdomen. When he became aware of a thought that distracted his attention from the breathing, he simply observed it, and gently brought the awareness back to the breathing.

As he did that and the body relaxed, he noticed the rhythm of the pulse of life. He shifted the attention to the sensations in the body.

He scanned his whole body part by part from head to toe. He felt tingling on some parts of the body, as if something was constantly changing.

He became so silent and still that he could almost hear the sound of the heartbeat. As he stayed in that state of observation, presence and stillness, his body totally relaxed, and he fell asleep.

He awoke to a sound outside his room. He looked at the clock, and it was the exact time to get up to go to dinner.

IN THE ESSENCE
In the essence of what we are,
There is no separation.
There is only that,
That I am.

CHAPTER 12

TO REMEMBER

While working at a social service agency, Pedro was invited to give a diversity talk at a volunteer training.

He started by saying:

"I'm the support group's coordinator for the Education and Support Services here at New Horizons. And I have an accent, just in case you haven't noticed."

Everybody laughed.

"That accent is just one small example of how people can be different.

"Training you about diversity essentially means helping you to understand, respect and appreciate those differences.

"One thing I like about New Horizons is the diversity of the organization. I also enjoy our willingness to confront our differences and debate issues together, until we come to a practical solution to a particular problem.

"I'd like to share with you something that I found very insightful in one of our Prevention Team meetings. Two of the staff members appeared to disagree on how to approach an issue.

"One of the staff members was a gay African American male, and the other was an Asian heterosexual female.

"I believe that the differences in their gender, cultural background and sexual orientation probably contributed to their different points of view. But it was not important to judge one right from wrong, but to allow these two different and valid points of view to see all the perspectives to help us arrive at a common goal.

"I recently attended a transgender and transsexual forum where I learned a lot about differences and being different.

"As an HIV positive and gay man, I thought that I already knew about being different. But the transgender individuals I met at that conference taught me what really being different is all about.

"One of the panelists mentioned that if they could put together all the tears they had cried for being different, it would overflow Lake Michigan.

"If we as individuals learn to appreciate, respect and embrace differences, then we are creating a more caring and loving world.

"I'm an optimist, so I can see the day when big private corporations would have at the end of a job listing 'transgender and transsexual individuals encouraged to apply.

"But, I also believe that it all starts with us. When we truly value ourselves, then society will value us.

"I'd like to share with you a little story of a woman named Ayla from the book "The *Clan of the Cave Bear*".

"She is essentially a breed apart. She has made an evolutionary jump forward. She possesses skills that only males are allowed to practice. Obviously, she is feared and is banished from the tribe. But she survives, alone in the wilderness. She copes and believes in herself. She returns to the tribe where she is finally accepted as a leader.

"The message here again is that she was different. She was seen as a threat because she upset the accepted norm. She represented change, and therefore was cast out instead of being acknowledged for her talents as a valuable resource to benefit the whole group.

"If you have studied Eastern philosophy, you may already embrace the concept of the balance of forces in the universe. In Eastern philosophy, there is no life without death. There is no spring without winter. You cannot appreciate the light without darkness. Without differences, there is only sameness. Without positives and negatives pulling against each other, there is no spark, no energy.

"Visionary business leaders also believe this. They believe in the concept of dynamic tension. They do not expect all people to like each other, only to work well together. They do not want all people to agree with each other, or with them. They do expect all people to celebrate their differences and to cooperate for a common goal.

"People who feel good about themselves see things in terms of new challenges and opportunities, and their minds wonder, 'What can I learn from this new situation?'

"And finally, I would like to say that it is our wish and goal that through this training you will learn to understand, respect and appreciate differences and each other."

As part of his work, Pedro also gave lectures and talks on HIV and AIDS education. He became a spokesperson for people living with HIV and AIDS. He spoke at different universities and organizations throughout the city.

In spite of all of Pedro's challenges with immigration and his HIV status, Pedro was able to remain in the United States legally. His lawyer had told him that the door was not only shut, but also locked due to his HIV status. Getting legal status in the United States with his condition was an impossible dream. But Pedro already knew very well about impossible dreams.

A year after getting his residency card, he became a best-selling author. He agreed to fly to Seattle, Washington to promote his latest book.

He was invited to do a presentation and a book signing at a local bookstore. At the end of the book signing, as he was getting ready to leave, he heard someone say, "There is one more book to sign."

Pedro looked up, and standing right in front of him was Luis.

Pedro did not recognize him at first. He was a lot older, but still as handsome as he was the last time Pedro saw him at the graduation ceremony.

Pedro asked, "Luis?"

"I wanted you to sign this copy for me. But most of all, I wanted to know if you were available this time to go to that dinner I asked you to so long ago. It looks like we both have waited long enough, don't you think?"

Pedro stood up with teary eyes and said, "I think I could make some room in my schedule." They burst into laughter and embraced each other.

As they embraced, a few people still there from the book signing who overheard their conversation started applauding.

A woman who didn't understand what was happening asked her friend, "What's that all about?" Her friend turned to her and told her, "That is Luis, the guy he talks about in his book."

Pedro finished gathering the rest of his belongings, and they walked to a restaurant a couple of blocks from where Pedro was presenting.

After they sat and took a few minutes to look over the menu, Pedro asked Luis, "What became of your life?"

"Well, I got married trying to please others and hoping that it would help me change. But I learned that there is nothing one can do to change his or her sexual orientation. Trying to do that is like wanting the sky to be green, when in fact it is blue. I was living the double life of blue in green, but I could no longer do that.

"I don't regret my marriage because it gave me two wonderful and beautiful children. My ex-wife remarried, and now we're very good friends. My daughter is still in college. My son is married and has two boys, so I'm also a grandfather," he said proudly.

Smiling, Pedro told him, "You're the most handsome grandfather I have ever seen.

"How did you know about the presentation or was it a coincidence that you were there?"

"Well, the universe works in mysterious ways to bring it all together," Luis said.

"Life is better organized than we could ever think it.

"I'm here visiting my son and his family. And, as I was sitting at a café finishing up reading your book, I spotted a flyer about the event, and the rest is history.

"So tell me about you?" Luis asked him.

Pedro waited for a second, smiled and said, "So much has happened since that last time we saw each other.

"I guess, it was never promised to be easy. But, if you already read the book, you pretty much know all about it." Pedro laughed.

Five months after that encounter, Pedro and Luis decided to move together to Seattle to be closer to the grandchildren.

* * *

"And that is the end of that story my young friend," the old man said.

"Was Pedro real?" the young man asked.

"You are Pedro," the old man responded.

"So, does that mean that you are Don Gregorio?"

"There is no separation," the old man replied.

"I don't understand," the young man said.

"What is there to understand? It's not so much about understanding, as it is to remember," the old man told him.

* * *

Vancouver – Present Day

When the young man comes back home from school for the first time, he goes to visit the old man. As he approaches the house, he sees it being demolished.

He asks one of the workers, "What happened to the old man who lived there?"

"Nobody has lived there for years," the man responds.

"I don't understand," he tells the man.

"What is there to understand?" the man asks.

THE BEGINNING

THE PROCESS

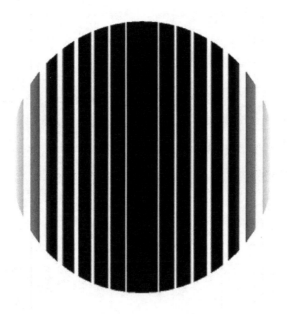

ONE
I am one with the light
I am one with the sky
I am one with the sun
I am one with the moon
I am one with me
I am one with you
I am one…

THE AUTHOR

Born in Venezuela, Argenis Vegas immigrated to the U.S. at the age of 21. He graduated from Northeastern Illinois University. He worked at City Colleges of Chicago, Jewish Vocational Services, and Horizons Community Services (now known as Center on Halsted).

During his years in social services, Vegas served as a member of the Chicago Area HIV Service Planning Council and volunteered with The Salvation Army, AIDS Alternative Health Project, Test Positive Aware Network, National Catholic AIDS Network, and AIDS Pastoral Care Network.

Not subscribing to any one particular spiritual discipline or tradition, Vegas has completed five levels of the Shambhala training, as well as the Sacred Path. He staffed all five levels and coordinated the Sacred Path for one year at The Shambhala Meditation Center in Chicago.

Vegas attended programs at Tassahara Mountain Zen Center in California, the City Zen Center in San Francisco and Green Gulch Farm Zen Center in Sausalito, California. He attended several Vipassana courses at Pakasa Meditation Center in Illinois and Vipassana Meditation Center in Venezuela. He has participated in the monastic winter retreats at the Mid-America Buddhist Association (MABA) in Missouri.

Vegas has been inspired by Rumi's wisdom and poems, as well as by Lao Tzu's "Tao Te Ching." He likes to study the laws of science and spirituality. He values and respects different points of view.

IN UNITY WE LOVE
IN SEPARATION WE FEAR

BOOK ORDERING INFORMATION

You can order directly from the publisher

by visiting:

www.createspace.com/4799213

For more information you can write to e-mail:

aovd1959@yahoo.com

Made in the USA
Middletown, DE
25 July 2015